Contents

A guide to living without power and water.

My goal is to help you remain safe and reasonably comfortable in your own home without power or water with items you most likely have available.

The following is based on the things I have learned while living through several hurricanes in southern Florida. When I got tired of that I moved to North Carolina and got to enjoy another hurricane and in the following years, Ice storms. Through all that I learned several things to make life easier.

The author is a Eagle Scout, Ham radio operator

and a Basic firearms safety instructor

written by Dana G.

first edition 1987, latest revision 02/2014

The disclaimer

Not everything in this book will work for everyone in every situation. It is your responsibility to determine which are safe and legal in your situation and area. All information contained in this book is for use at your own risk.

"All you need to survive is water, food, and shelter. Everything else is a luxury."

What I do when the power goes out.

If you have some notice of incoming weather you will find it much easier to do things before the power goes out.

First thing to do is what you should do in any survival situation. Don't panic, and take stock of your situation.

Do I have enough drinking water? Enough for 3 days?(one gallon per day, per person.)

Is there food in the house? Enough for 3 days?

Locate your flashlight and check batteries and put it where you can find it in the dark, oil lamps and camping coolers.

Have a generator? Do I have enough gas and check the oil in the engine, gather up extension cords and locate your gas siphon. Then I'll go fill up the vehicle and my gas cans. If I need more gas than I have in the gas cans, my truck's fuel tank holds 30 gallons that I can get to with a gas siphon.

Pick up some ice or empty your ice maker into a cooler, and pick up a few groceries that don't need refrigeration while you're out, if it looks like its going to be awhile before you get power back.

Fill up all the oil lamps and the kerosene heater if it's cold outside and don't forget the extra blankets.

Is my rain barrel or cistern at least half full,so I can flush the commode without using good drinking water. If not or you don't have one.

Fill up the tub so you'll have water to flush the commode and have a bucket handy to transfer water. If your tub slowly leaks out the drain with the drain pulled like mine does, than get and put a rubber stopper over the drain also.

Can I drink the water in the tub? That's a matter of personal choice, if you clean the tub before you fill it up it'll be OK, if it's got a tub ring and soap scum thick enough to write your name in, it may not be such a good idea to drink.

Once you have everything ready and going. Relax for this will be over soon enough.

My priorities once the power is out.

<u>Heating water for coffee and cooking.</u>

Heat, A normal kerosene heater. I put wood blocks or a scrap piece of carpet under my heater to keep from messing up the floor. Also shown, two cell phones and a L.E.D. TV that are being powered by the inverter and battery in the next picture.

Power, a simple inverter setup I use for several hours before I get out the generator. I normally don't even get the generator out and going until the power is out for at least 4 hours.

Items to have on hand

Knife and Knife sharpener

Multitool

Extra gasoline, kerosene, or propane

Hatchet, small ax, or a small tree saw

Signal mirror or a CD can be used also

Lighters or Matches in waterproof case

Tarp 6'x10' for water collection, shelter or roof repair

Fire starter sticks

Lightweight rope or twine

Water purifying tablets/unscented bleach

Hand sanitizer or soap if you have water

Small or folding shovel

Toilet paper (take half used rolls, flatten and put inside zip lock bags for carry)

Duct tape (use whole rolls in home/car, wrap 6' around a dowel for carry)

Compass/GPS

Whistle metal

Blanket small (4'x 6' size slice hole in middle to put head through)

Poncho (wear over blanket to keep warm and dry)

Canteen or water container

Container to boil water in

Fire extinguishers

Flashlight, Candles

Oil lamps and lamp oil

Simple cook kit from army surplus store

(optional) Radio frequency scanner

(optional) 12volt cooler for car

(optional) Generator

(optional) 12volt to 115volt power inverter

The above items are things that I have used on a regular basis when I didn't have power or water. Most items you may already have, just locate them and make sure they are still functional. You will need to try some of the techniques and see which items and methods work best for your needs.

Knives and Multitools

Before the hurricanes in Florida I carried the normal non-lock back knife with a 2-2.5" blade. When the power is out and the water is off, your knife is your best friend. I stumbled through the first hurricane. After that I became the proud owner of a lock-back knife with the one hand opening feature and a good thick blade 3.5" long.

In a survival situation a knife is used for cutting, prying, chopping and eating It becomes an extension of your hand. I now have several.

For daily carry I have a folding lock-back with a 3" blade. For use when things go downhill I carry a full tang knife (a full tang blade is where you can see the metal of the blade because it extends the full width and length of the handle) with a 4" blade. Serrated blades are a personal choice. If you will be cutting a lot of vines or rope they are great. The only problem is they can be a pain to sharpen.

A good knife can be used to chop tree limbs by putting the knife blade against the wood and hitting the back of the blade with another piece of wood.

It would be a better idea to get a hatchet (small ax) for minor chopping.

I looked at several of those Rambo style survival knives with the hollow handles while they look impressive, none of the ones I saw were worth spending your money on. Unless someone gives you one don't even bother.

Knife sharpeners

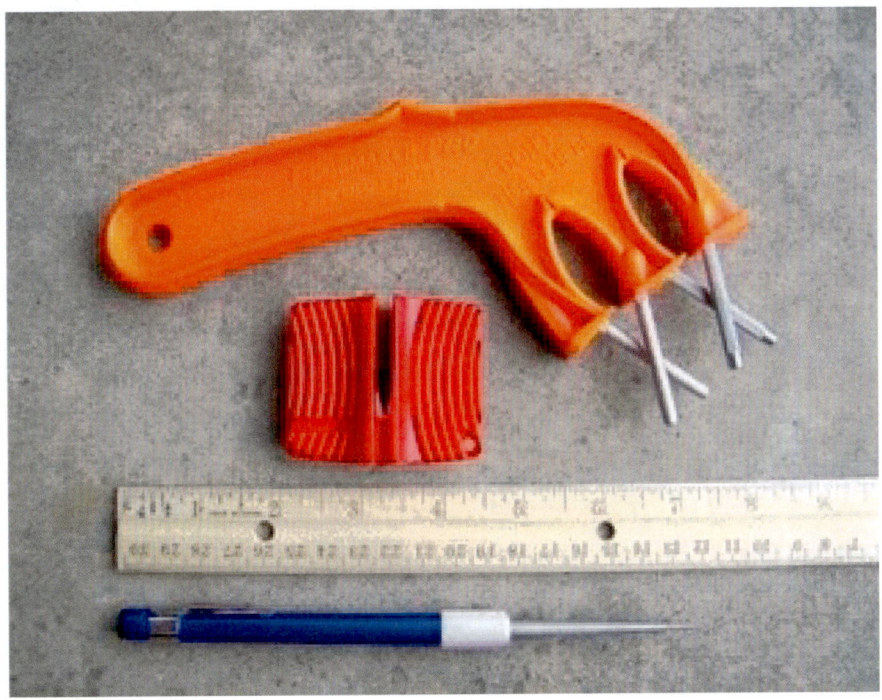

    Knife sharpeners; just make sure you have one. They don't have to be fancy they come in all sizes and shapes, they can be ceramic, carbide or diamond coated rods. I keep several around with a preference for the smaller ones in the car or truck and a larger one in the house with a big handle.

    Look in the fishing or camping section for the small ones and in the kitchen section for the bigger ones, don't buy an electric sharpener for use when the power is out, all it takes is 3-7 strokes through a sharpener to give you a nice edge. Priced from $2.00-$12.00

Multitools

These have got to be the greatest thing since Electricity.

Things to look for. The first is quality. Extend the pliers and squeeze the handles do they feel solid enough? Remember you're not going to be rebuilding your car engine just trying to get a better grip in stuff.

MAKE SURE IT HAS A CAN OPENER. You are most likely with out power.

After you get your multitool try out all of its blades. Does the can opener work, which means you actually open a can of soup with it so that you understand how to do the hook, punch through, move and repeat method of opening a can. Make sure the wire cutters on the pliers will cut a wire clothes hanger and softer stranded wire like on a lamp cord. Can you put some pressure on the screw drivers with out bending them? The knife blade is it long and thin if so sharpen it to a fine edge this will be used for more delicate work.

Expect to pay at least $30 and up for a quality Multitool depending on the number of blades and **make sure it has a can opener**.

I would also recommend the addition of a couple of manual can openers to your kitchen inventory. They are not expensive and they do break.

Fire Starting

Tip: Go to the big box store and buy a few packages of disposable lighters with several in it and put two individual lighters in the trunk/glove compartment of every car, put some in the house in every drawer or cabinet that can't be reached by children, presto no more fire starting problems.

Keep matches, lighters and fire starting material in your home at all times. Store them in a water proof container even in your home. I use a Tupperware style sandwich container. In with the matches I keep a lighter and some fire starter sticks from the camping section of the local store.

In the vehicles I keep a lighter and a couple of fire sticks wrapped up in a zip lock bag, nice and simple.

When keeping matches in a watertight match case it's a good idea to put in a section of the striker strip from the match box.

BATTERY AND STEEL WOOL Take a piece of steel wool without soap and connect it to both sides of a 9-volt battery. I have found that unrolling the steel wool and adding paper then rolling it back up, before using the battery is a very quick way to get it burning. Once the steel wool is burning gently blow on the paper wrapped in the steel wool. Use this small flame to set your tinder ablaze. This method is easy especially when done with a 9-volt battery. Other size battery's D, C, A, AA or AAA will be more difficult. (using this method on a larger battery, like a car, is dangerous and not recommended.).

MAGNESIUM FIRE STARTER Have the advantage of being able to still spark and ignite when damp and can be stored for years without degrading. This is something I would highly recommend a practice run with to get the hang of it, before you have to do this in the dark when you are cold and wet.

TINDER The stuff used to keep the fire burning long enough to get the smaller wood burning. Were do I find dry tinder in my house? That would be newspaper, telephone books, dryer lint, toilet paper and junk mail torn into strips.

FIRE STICKS (store bought tinder) These are made of compressed sawdust and some sort of wax. They generally come in packs of 12 with instructions to use 1-2 complete sticks to light a fire, for me this seems a bit much because a 1" piece of fire stick will give you a useable fire starting flame for about 5 minutes.

Always build your fire in a safe place. Keep your fire small or you will attract unwanted visitors or neighbors looking for food, water and shelter. Unless you plan to feed and warm the entire block keep fires small and cooking smells to a minimum.

It's recommended you keep at least 2 fire extinguishers per floor with a minimum rating of 2A:10BC ($20.00) with a preference for a higher rating such as a 3A: 40BC ($25.00) in your home for a survival situation. For the car or kitchen it's recommended you have at least a 5BC ($10.00) rated fire extinguisher. Have battery operated smoke detectors, these two items are the cheapest insurance you will ever buy. Remember you will be using open flames and may be dealing with gas or kerosene during a power outage.

Basic first aid items

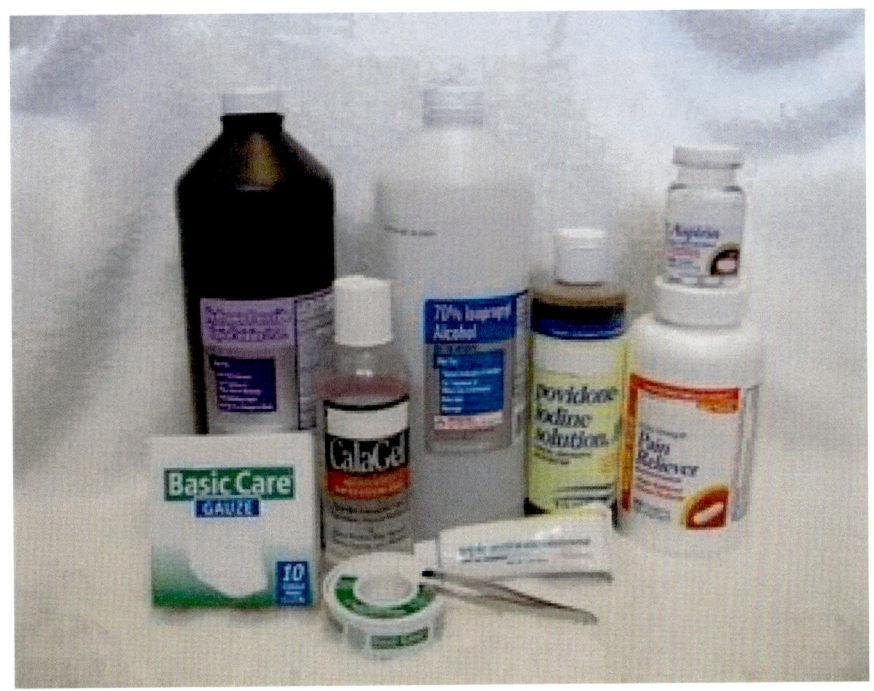

Your first aid kit should include at a minimum the following items,

peroxide,

rubbing alcohol,

iodine,

aspirin or Tylenol,

antibiotic cream,

anti-itching cream,

assorted band aids,

first aid tape,

gauze pads in various sizes,

tweezers,

and a cold compress (or ice in a zip lock bag)

Ace elastic bandage

Antacid

Latex gloves

Magnifying glass

Super glue

Try to have available hand sanitizer that doesn't require water.

Most of what you will be dealing with is cuts, scrapes, bruising, splinters, sunburn, bug bites or stings and unknown rashes.

Finding water

-Ice Maker

-Hot Water Heater

-Fill up bathtub (should be done before hand)

-Tank on back of commode

-Cistern / rain barrels (need to purify/boil)

-Fish Tanks / koi pond (need to purify/boil)

-Ice and snow(winter only option)

You must have water for drinking and cooking. Figure one gallon per person per day as a minimum. For example a family of four, 4 people at 4 gallons per day times three days equals twelve gallons of drinkable water.

Will I use a gallon of water a day?

If you are outside clearing debris from your yard fully expect to use twice this much per day. If you are inside just waiting for the power to come back on you might only use half this amount.

The tank on the back of the commode (don't drink the water out of the bowl). Be careful when dipping water out of the back of a commode as there is generally sediment in the bottom of a commode tank expect 1.5 to 2 gallons of water. **Don't do this if you have toilet bowl cleaners hanging in the water tank.**

The ice maker. Take all the ice in the ice maker bin and put in a pot or bowl and let it melt.

A hot water heater. To get at this water you will need to first turn off the power to the hot water heater. But the power is already off? If you get power back before you get water, you will be the proud owner of new hot water heater elements or a whole new hot water heater. When you get power back make sure you have water flowing from the hot water side of the faucet before you turn the hot water heater back on.

Locate a garden hose and a bucket or pot to catch water in, attach the garden hose to the hose valve located somewhere near the bottom of the tank and have the other end in the bucket. Be careful as most hot water heaters will keep water hot for up to a week with out power. You may need to open the hot water side of a faucet in the house to release the vacuum in the hot water tank. Expect 30-40 gallons of water depending on the size of your hot water tank

Be sure to test this valve before you need it as hot water heaters can build up sediment in the bottom of the tank which is what the drain is really for.

Take note of what kind of drain valve handle you have, the older hot water heaters have a normal faucet handle as seen below. The newer hot water heaters have a child proof faucet handle that requires the use of a flat blade screwdriver to open.

I keep a special separate piece of water hose rolled up with the ends screwed together to keep bugs and such out of the hose just for this purpose.

Other options are pools, ponds, lakes, rivers, dehumidifiers, and rain water none of which I would drink with out boiling or treating with iodine tabs. For pools, ponds, lakes, and rivers find you a clean bucket take and dip into the water, you don't want to have to walk too far as water weighs about 8 pounds per gallon. For rain water make a simple cistern out of a bucket or barrel under a rain gutter downspout or the window a/c unit, be sure to empty these on a regular basis or you will be a mosquito farmer.

Shown Above: A shed, some gutter and a 110 gal. Stock tank. It's that easy.

In the following picture you will see my solution to the mosquitoes living in the water. If you do go the fish option make sure the tank is in the shade or the water will get too hot and kill the fish. All I need now is some lilly pads and I will have a koi pond, which may be a solution if you live in one of the areas that is against rainwater harvesting.

Please note you still have to feed the fish daily with regular fish food.

For my fish I purchased about a dozen of the feeder goldfish $0.15 each, when I got them they were about an inch long, now they are about twice that long.

This is another cistern I built using an old heating oil drum. While I won't drink this water because it still has a slight odor of kerosene, it is good for flushing commodes and washing your hands after working on the car. Be aware that in the cold of winter it can freeze and crack the tank.

In winter time don't forget the ice and snow option. Bring inside and let melt at room temperature. Or use a camp stove or fire, remember that snow will burn if you try to melt it to fast. Don't eat or melt yellow snow.

If you have a flood situation you can use the flood water to flush a commode as long as the water is slow moving and can be approached safely. Flushing a commode with flood water will not work if the flood waters are near the same elevation as your home. Because the flood waters fill up the sewer lines.

DO NOT drink flood water even if you boil, filter, or use iodine tablets for any reason. You have no idea how much sewage or chemicals it may contain. This will not work if there is flood water up to your home.

It's better to be thirsty and well than hugging the great white stool and feeling like you're going to die from drinking bad water.

Purifying water

Do not attempt to drink water that has a oil like sheen on it or has a chemical smell. The methods of water treatment discussed here will NOT remove oils or chemicals

The simplest is to bring to a boil and keep boiling for 5 minutes then let cool and enjoy. The water may have a flat taste after boiling, this can be improved on by putting the water in a container and giving it a good shaking.

Another option is to use iodine tabs normally found in the camping section. The brand I have used required me to put 2 tablets in a quart of water and wait 30 minutes. They do make the water taste odd and some have a warning about not using for long term and if you are pregnant or nursing.

There are other options for purifying water involving filters/life straws($20-$40); you can find these at Amazon.com and other stores specializing in hiking, camping or the outdoors. These are far more advanced than the filters that you use to make tap water taste better. Part of their purpose is to remove the things that the water treatment plant removes from the water for you.

How do I treat water?

It is not necessary to treat water from a public water supply if it is already chlorinated. Unless a boil alert has been issued.

Clorox - Amounts according to civil defense guidelines. Double if water is cloudy. After adding proper dosage, stir and allow to stand about 30 minutes.

Quart water – add 2 drops bleach

½ Gallon water – add 4 drops bleach

1 Gallon water – add 16 drops bleach

5 Gallons water – add 1 tsp bleach

Essentials of a water treatment kit -

1 bottle Clorox (Clorox will loose it's "oomph" after about 18 months, so this needs to be rotated. Do

Not use scented bleach.)
1 tsp measure
1 medicine dropper
1 funnel
Coffee filters (these would be for filtering water with debris).

Boiling - Most water can be purified for drinking purposes by boiling it for 5 to 10 minutes.

Purification Tablets - Tablets that release iodine may be used safely to purify drinking water.

Personal water filter - Life straw and Sawyer are the two brands I have.

Flushing a commode with a bucket of water.

The power and water may be off but you can still flush a commode. How's this possible? All household drains are based on gravity, water always flows downhill. This will not work during flood conditions outside your home. Which if there is that much water outside or under your home you probably shouldn't be there anyway.

There are two ways to flush a commode with a bucket of water.

Fill up the tank on the back of your commode and push the handle as normal. Be sure to fill the tank to the top of the overflow tube.

Or you can hold a bucket of water about waist high and pour slowly into the middle of the toilet bowl until all solids are gone and you (may) hear the drain gurgle. Then add a bit more water to cover the bottom hole in the toilet bowl. This keeps sewer smells from seeping into the house. This is something that should have a practice run as it takes about 3 gallons of water for a complete flush. Try not to use good drinking water for this purpose. It is best to use water from creeks, ponds, or rain water for this purpose.

Try to minimize flushing of the commode by remembering this saying

If it's brown flush it down, if its yellow let it mellow.

If you have a situation where you are looking after several people or have very limited supply of flushing water. You may have to have all adults urinate in a bucket and use this to flush the commode. Make sure you have a lid for the bucket and keep it outside as this will have a strong smell. Make sure you have 2.5-3 gallons for a complete flush.

Don't forget the next option and that would be the bucket, poo pit or the outhouse. Dig a hole 1-3 feet deep and fashion a support to sit on with a hole in the middle. After each pooing sprinkle some dirt over the poo. Be careful with buckets and small children, you don't want them to fall in and drown. Keep a lid on the bucket when not in use for safety and to keep the smell in or put in a trash bag and twist the bag closed when not in use. Put the bucket up against a wall or the edge of the tub to keep it from sliding out from under you. Test this before you need to go, as not all buckets will support your weight.

Cooking

--The powers out and I'm hungry. Now what?

Eat the perishable foods first. That means what ever has to be kept refrigerated or frozen. Try to keep the refrigerator doors closed as much as possible.

Expect things in the refrigerator to stay useable for 1-2 days, in the freezer 2-3 days. After 4-6 hours without power the refrigerator will slowly begin to warm up.

When the temperature outside is staying below 39 degrees I have put foods that need refrigeration out side in a shady spot in a cooler. I have also put items in the trunk of the car when temps are consistently below freezing. 12volt coolers that plug into the cars power sockets are available. These are not freezers just a cooler. You will have to start your car to recharge the cars battery every so often or leave it running depending on the model. Cost about $85.00 for a 40 quart size.

--I want a hot cup of coffee and / or a hot meal.

Got a gas grill or camp stove? Those pots and pans in the kitchen work just as good on a grill. BE CAREFULL USING the pots or pans with plastic handles they do melt!!!! Remember keep the flame down low until you get a feel for how fast your grill cooks with regular pots and pans.

Don't use any gas grills or camping stoves INDOORS, they use up the oxygen and can produce carbon monoxide which will kill you.

--I don't have a grill or camp stove. Now what?

Do you have a kerosene heater?

See if a tea pot or frying pan will sit on top. I have used kerosene heaters to heat water in a tea pot for a cup of instant coffee or instant noodles and have used small pots to heat up a can of soup. Be sure to have a hot pot mitt handy, the kerosene heater will heat up the whole pot, handle and all. This is a sloooow method but it works.

The next option that I have used is to build a small fire. Round up some cinder blocks, red bricks, stepping stones or some big rocks (don't use rocks that have been in rivers, creeks, ponds or water as they may hold water, that will cause them to explode when heated) get the oven rack from the oven and lay it across the supports you have set up and presto open flame grilling. You may have to scrape the dirt away under the supports to get your grill to sit level. Don't use the racks out of a refrigerator as many are coated with plastic or sealer to prevent rust.

--What's the easiest thing to cook?

Anything that falls under the title of heat and eat. This would be almost anything that comes packed in a can as these items are often precooked or pasteurized as part of the canning process.

Don't forget the food in the refrigerator. Things you'll commonly find in my refrigerator / freezer are hamburgers, hot dogs, eggs, cheese, sandwich meats, steaks, ice cream, frozen pizza. Make a sandwich meat and cheese omelet for breakfast, hamburgers, hot dogs and ice cream for lunch and steak and eggs for dinner.

Frozen pizza can be a little bit of trouble. I normally use the pizza tray and place some tin foil over the pizza lightly so it doesn't stick to the cheese. Sometimes they cook just fine other times they take forever.

A package of instant noodles, I find myself eating a lot of these because they are so easy, all you do is heat water and add the water to the noodles and wait 5-10 minutes.

If your short on water, eat out of the same pan you cooked in or heat food in the can it came in. You'll need a hot pot holder or some pliers to grip the top edge of the can so you don't burn your self.

To save on dirty dishes. Use up any paper plates, plastic forks and paper cups you may have to help save on dishes piling up in the sink.

-- I've got water but no power and dishes are piling up.

Stop up your sink drain. Boil up some water with your grill/kerosene heater, pour in your sink slowly to avoid splashing and add some cool water until you can comfortably put your hands in the water. If you have a double bowl sink put hot water in the second bowl and you can wash in warm water and rinse in hot water. Put a towel on the counter to drain you dishes on.

Lighting

----The power is out. How do I see?

-Open the blinds and curtains - oil lamps – flashlights – candles

Open the blinds and curtains during the day. I'm putting this in because I have a teenager that would walk around with a flashlight during the day and didn't realize that light also comes from the sun and not just a light switch.

The easiest are flashlights. Make sure you have batteries that work in your flashlight before it gets dark and keep up with were you put your flashlight.

If you are like me and you store dead batteries in your flashlight, then check out the flashlights that have a hand crank or you shake to generate power without the use of batteries. The ones with a hand crank put out more light and cost more. The ones that you shake put out enough light to get you to the bathroom and back without tripping over the kid's toys and the dog. They won't focus a beam of light on the moon like some battery flashlights will, however they will light up a 2-3 foot circle from 6 feet away. Can be found at Amazon.com and local mega stores. $10.00-$20.00

Oil lamps are not just for looks. They are great when the power is out and they are also good for candlelight dinners.

Oil lamps are relatively inexpensive, they sell for $5-$10.00 each depending on size.

In our home they are in plain sight as decoration. We have four in the living room, one in the bathroom, two in the kitchen and one in the adult's room.

All are kept ¾ full of the proper lamp oil (if you fill them completely they wick the lamp oil out slowly around the threaded neck).

When you get home with your lamp it is a good idea to trim the wick into an upside down u shape. This will make the flame burn more evenly. Go ahead and give it a test burn to understand how to properly adjust the flame.

Fill up lamps outside. You will need to purchase the special lamp oil to use in them. In our store it's on the shelf right below the lamps. After you get them filled clean up any drips and let them dry off if any lamp oil has spilled, a small funnel will make the filling process easier.

To light the lamps you will need to remove the glass chimney cover and light the exposed tip of the wick, adjust the flame height to about a half an inch. Then replace the glass chimney it will create a chimney effect and make the flame bigger. You will need to turn down the flame or it will smoke up the inside of the glass. The glass chimney is a bit difficult to clean without a long handled kitchen or bottle brush.

I generally get 8-10 hours of burn time before I refill them.

To turn them off lower the wick all the way. Some can be blown out by blowing across the top of the glass chimney, don't touch the glass chimney while the flame is burning. It will burn you, just trust me from experience.

Candles are another ever popular option. They don't need batteries. Have an unlimited shelf life. Just be careful as it is an open flame.

Glow sticks are not really a good option for power outages. They generally have a two year shelf life, are only good for one 8-10 hour period, and cost around a $1.00 each.

DO NOT USE CAMPING LANTERNS INDOORS AS THEY PRODUCE CARBON MONOXIDE WHICH CAN KILL YOU IN AN ENCLOSED SPACE.

Generators

When the power is out and you have a generator all you do is start it up and plug in your refrigerator, the TV and a couple of lamps then everything is good again.

What to look for in a generator. The one with the best and biggest muffler, they are loud when running. They all have plugs that look like the ones in a house. Some generators are little some are big and all of them are rated by watts.

The easiest way to figure out what you need to run one refrigerator, one TV and 2-3 lamps is base it on one 20 amp circuit (20 amps X 115 volts = 2300 running watts) so you would look for a generator with a rating of at least 2300 running watts. You will also see surge wattage. Surge wattage is the maximum wattage the generator can produce for less then 10 seconds. The surge wattage is needed to start the compressor in the refrigerator and the running wattage keeps the refrigerator running. Running wattage is the amount of wattage the generator can produce as long as you have gas in the tank.

Another way to figure what you need is to add up the power required for each item as shown the data plate of all electrical items, which can be hidden anywhere on an electrical item that you want to power.

Examples

(805w).....Refrigerator - 7 amps, 7 amps x 115 volts = 805 watts

(1400w)...Microwave - 1400 watts consumed-800 watt cooking

(180w).....3 lamps - 60 watt bulbs, 60 watts x 3 bulbs = 180

(80w).......TV - 80 watts

(10w).......DVD player - 10 watts

(161w).....Electric can opener - 1.4 amps, 1.4amps x 115 volts =161

(Total 2636 watts)

To run all of these items at the same time you will need to look for a generator with a RUNNING WATTAGE of greater than 2636 watts.

SURGE WATTAGE is what the generator can produce for a few seconds(for starting up electrical items)

RUNNING WATTAGE is what the generator can produce as long as there is fuel in it.

Generators are available in sizes up to 10,000 running watts at local home improvement stores and farm supply stores. Only buy what you need because it will be in storage until you need it. The generators I have used recommended that you run them at least once a year under load to make sure everything is working properly.

When running a generator for power do not run it in an enclosed area or a room attached to your home. Its exhaust contains carbon monoxide which at best will make you very sick or at worst will kill you. To keep your generator from walking off I recommend chaining it with a heavy chain and a strong lock to a sturdy post, tree, or some other solid object as generators can be worth their weight in gold during a power outage.

A generator in the 3000 to 5000 running watt range will use about 3-5 gallons of fuel every 8-10 hours depending on how much power is being used.

Running low on gas? Have a way to siphon gas?

Use the gas out of any lawnmower, tiller, ATV, etc. Don't forget the 2 stroke gas mix. It will work also, just expect some bluish smoke from the exhaust. I prefer using a gas siphon over sucking on the end of a hose, a mouth full of gas can ruin a perfectly good day.

Every generator I have used has required single weight oil of 30w, which if you don't have or run out of you can use multi weight 10w30 oil. I recommend getting some extra 30w oil as generators do use oil when under full load. Make sure the generator has a low oil shutdown feature.

Generators are loud even with the optional large muffler. Try to point the muffler exhaust port away from the house. It's a good idea to find out if your area has any noise restrictions after a certain time at night. In my experience the quiet time started between 9pm and 10pm.

You'll need plenty of extension cords. Do a test layout of the various items you plan to run. For example run an extension cord to the TV and refrigerator and some lights. Buy the best extension cords you can, a small skinny cord can over heat if used to run a refrigerator or a microwave.

Avoid running extension cords where they will get cut or pinched when a door is opened and closed or where they will be walked on or tripped over.

The generator shown has an additional 220 volt 20 amp twist lock plug. Notice it's also a 5750 running watts with a 7200 watt surge.

What can you run with a 20 amp 220 volt circuit? Do you use well water? This generator will run up to a 1.5 horsepower submersible deep well pump or a very large window a/c unit.

In my case it was used for power at two homes side by side with a total of 2 refrigerators, 1 freezer, several lamps, 3 TV's, a video game and a microwave and I now have enough extension cords for a construction site. The generator was kept chained to the bed of my pickup and once a day I would unplug everything and drive out to the well house and hook the generator to the well pump for 2-3 hours. This gave everyone time to get a (cold) shower, flush the commodes and give my neighbors time to come by and get buckets of water.

You will need to be an electrician or hire one or have an understanding of how to hook up 220 volt lines to do this. In my case my neighbor (an electrician) hard wired a second 220 line to the pump box with a plug to match the generator I had. After everything was over with we installed a double throw switch with a covered 220 plug in and I got a 220 volt extension cord/cable from a local RV dealer. Make sure the ends match your plug in's as there are several different combinations of plugs.

12 volt to 110 ac power inverters

A 12 volt dc to 110 volt ac power inverter. Does just what it says. It converts 12 volt dc auto power to standard ac house power.

The smaller ones plug directly into a cigarette lighter or a 12 volt accessory outlet in your auto and convert it to 110 ac household current, with a standard household plug, newer models may also have a USB charging port. $30 on Amazon.com

Inverters are rated in watts just like generators, common size's are from 100 watts to 1000 watts continuous with a surge wattage of about twice the running wattage. Inverters are great for running small electrical items.

Why only small electrical items? A 140 watt inverter will pull about 15 amps per hour from a 12 volt battery. A normal 550 CCA car battery has about 80 amp hours of reserve or storage, so 80 amp hours divided by 15 amps per hour equals 5.3 hours of run time at full inverter output before the battery may not start your car (80 / 15 = 5.3). My recommendation is to keep the car running while using any inverter. A 140 watt inverter won't run much, just a can opener and a small TV, about 20" or less in size also great for charging cell phones and laptops.

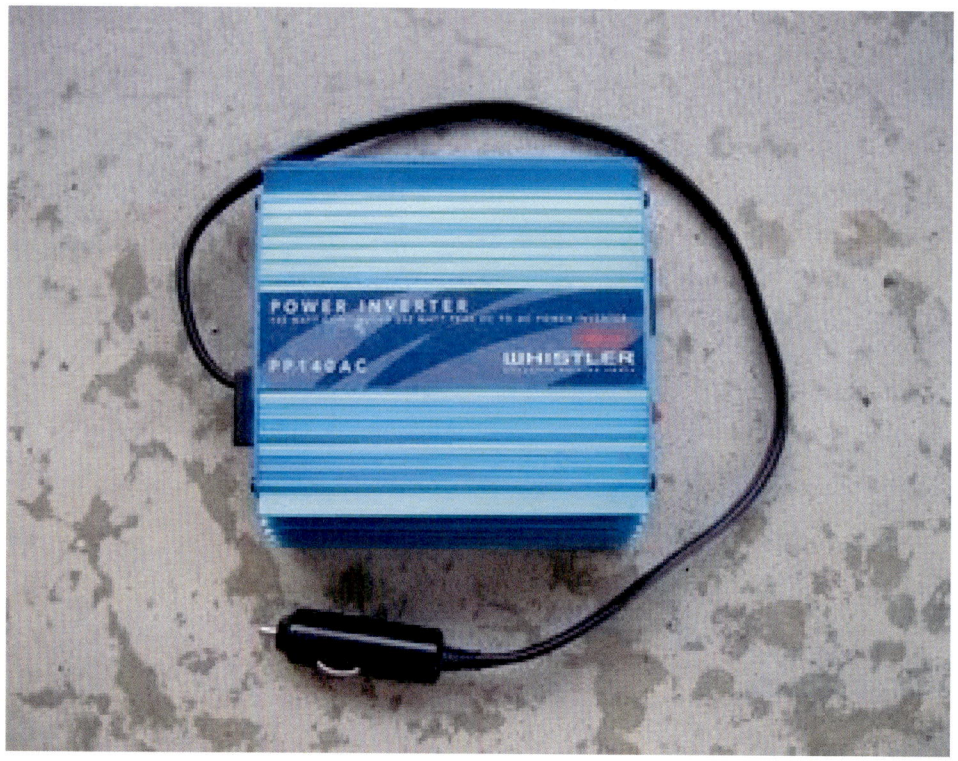

With larger inverters, lets say a 375 watt inverter, at full output it will pull about 40 amps per hour and has to be hooked directly to the battery, because wiring in a auto generally has a maximum rating of 20 amps and the 375 watt inverter pulls 40.

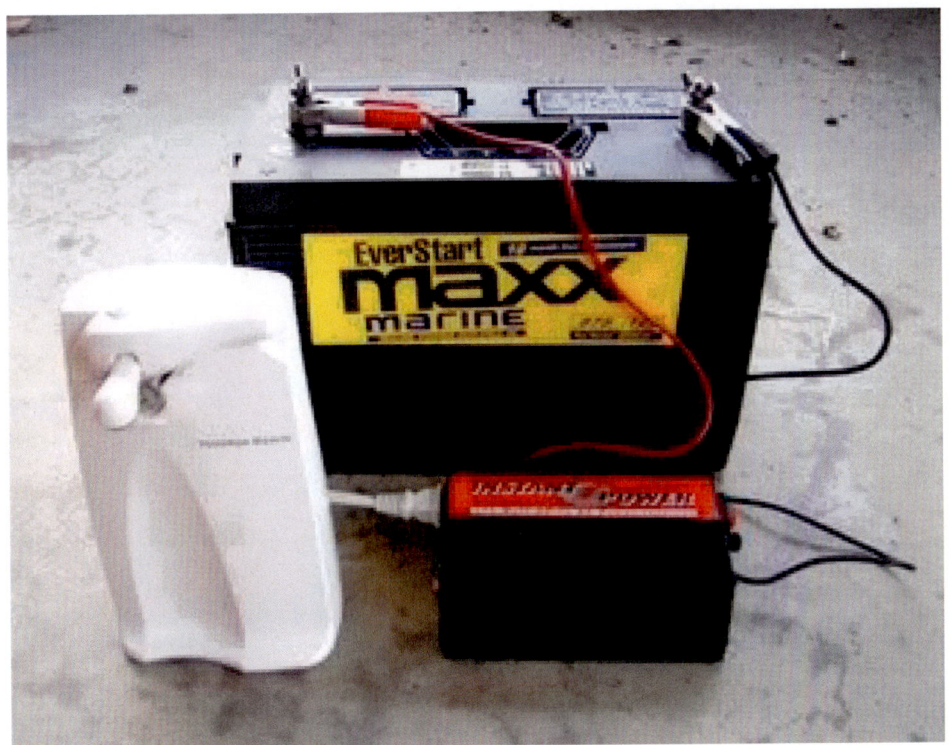

Before buying an inverter find out how many amps your car alternator is rated for. The amp rating maybe stamped on the outside of the alternator or just call the auto parts store and ask, of the alternators available for your auto what is the stock amp output and do they carry any with a higher output.

My oldest pickup a 1985 model has a factory alternator that is rated for 45 amps output, so using a 375 watt inverter pulling 40 amps will burn up the alternator wiring. I learned this the hard way. When I went to replace the alternator I asked if there was an alternator with a higher output. The answer was how many amps do you want. So now I have a 90 amp alternator, 45 amps for running the truck, 40 amps for the inverter and 5 amps for the ham radio and CB. Upgrading to an alternator with a higher output does cost more and you may have to upgrade the wiring from the alternator to the battery to handle the increased amp output.

My newer pickup comes standard with a 90 amp alternator it also has multiple 12 volt power outlets and according to the owners manual I can use up to 20 amps of extra power without harming the charging system.

     In the above picture is a trolling motor battery, a 375 watt inverter, and a battery tender(charger). During the most recent power outage this was used to power chargers for 2 cell phones, a tablet, and run a 39" L.E.D. TV. It provided power for 12 hours before the inverter auto shut down due to low battery voltage. So I started the truck and hooked up the inverter to the truck battery. You can also recharge the battery by hooking jumper cables to the trolling motor battery from the truck battery while the truck is running.

This battery is kept charged and maintained with the battery tender until needed when the power is on.

This is a simple solar charging setup I use to keep the other battery charged. The solar setup is a 30 watt solar panel, a morningstar 4.5 amp charge controller, mounting brackets, clamps, and a car battery that will still hold a charge.

It will keep the battery fully charged if you need to charge cell phones, run a small inverter hooked to a small T.V. or small appliance or jump start a car. Once the battery is drained of power the inverter will shut off and all you can do is charge cell phones with a 12volt car charger using just the solar panel as long as the solar panel is still hooked to the battery.

Where to go if you are forced to leave your home

If you are forced to leave your home because your home has become unlivable due to rising water, wildfire, fallen tree damage or possibly large pieces of your home are missing.

Your options are leave and go to a shelter, go stay with friends or family, hotel or motel, setup a tent or camper in the back yard, sleep in your car or truck.

Sleeping in your car or truck is OK for one or two nights, will not work if you have a family.

Setup a tent or camper in the back yard nice and simple, you can keep an eye on things. If your home is only lightly damaged you may still be able to get at your foodstuffs and any water supply's that you have.

Hotel or motel just trying to find one with an empty room will be a problem. Before any money changes hands verify they have running water and power.

Go stay with friends or family. Try to contact them first, they maybe in worse shape than you are. Take all of the supplies that you can. When it's all over you may never want to see them again.

Go to a shelter. Unless you have no other option I would avoid this. You will have no sleep, no privacy, no personal space and your stuff may grow legs when you are not looking. However they do provide you with food, water, some medical care and a place to sit or lie down.

I have to leave my home

is there anything I can do to save what's left?

If possible turn off the incoming water and turn off the power at your main breaker.

Why? The power and water is already off? As soon as possible there will be crews working to restore utilities.

In the case of water service your water pipes will go from zero pressure/psi (pounds per square inch) to around 40-60psi in a short period of time. Any weak spots in your plumbing from age or damage due to the current situation may start leaking. A faucet may have been left on and a sink or tub overflows. A couple inches of water throughout your home will lead to an incredible amount of problems with mold, mildew, electrical shorts, having to replace carpet, flooring and possible structural damage from wood rot.

In freezing conditions after you turn off the water and power you should drain the plumbing system as best you can, to prevent the water in the pipes from freezing and bursting open a pipe.

To drain your plumbing first make sure the water service to your home is cut off at the incoming line preferably at the street or water meter. Double check to make sure the power is off at the main circuit breaker and to be on the safe side I also cut off the breaker to the hot water heater (the elements in the hot water heater will overheat and fail and possibly cause a fire if not kept immersed in water when the power comes back on).

Now open a water faucet at the lowest point in your home. I prefer an outside hose faucet so I don't have to worry about what to do with the 5-20 gallons of water that drains out. Now go inside and open all faucets hot and cold in the kitchen, bathroom, laundry room (you may need to loosen the hoses behind the washer, be sure to tighten these back up before you turn on the water) and flush the commode if possible so that the tank on the back and the bowl has as little water as possible in it. For extreme low temperature a cup full of RV water line antifreeze, different from car antifreeze and can be found at RV dealers, tractor/farm supply stores and the camping section of some larger stores, cost $4-$8.00 per gallon) can be put in the bowl and tank, do not let animals or people drink from this water.

The hot water heater will have to be drained separately. To do this attach a garden hose to the drain valve and turn on the valve. Make sure the other end of the garden hose is lower than the hot water tank and outside or in a suitable drain. When draining hot water heaters be careful of the remaining hot water as some hot water tanks will keep the water hot without power for up to a week.

In the case of power service when it is restored it is common for there to be power surges which can damage anything you plug in to a power outlet. If your home has sustained any damage from water or structural damage there may be a short in the wiring which can cause a fire when the power is restored. I also recommend unplugging anything and everything.

Don't forget to empty out your refrigerator and freezer it will stink when you get back.

Lock your doors when you leave, to help prevent looting.

What do I take if forced to leave my home?

When you have to leave your home there's a good chance the clothes you're wearing will be worn and slept in for a week or more. They need to be comfortable and allow freedom of movement. For example loose fitting jeans and a belt, sturdy shoes and socks that are comfortable to walk or stand in for long periods of time. The lines at stores with power, shelters and soup kitchens can be very long.

Carry or wear something with long sleeves this will help protect you from the sun, cold or mosquitoes depending on where and why you had to leave. Don't forget a hat suitable for the conditions.

Dress for the coldest nighttime temperatures you will encounter at that time. You can always remove clothes to cool off during the day. In shelter situations bring a backpack and keep it with you at all times, when you remove a layer of clothing don't lay it down, put it immediately into your backpack. Don't forget Chap Stick and any medicines you may need.

Leaving on foot, don't expect to carry much, unless you're used to hiking on a regular basis. A gallon of water is about 8lbs, box of dry cereal and some energy bars 2lbs, some cans of food with a pull top and crackers 2lbs, some blankets 2lbs, and your basic survival kit (knife, multitool, and flashlight) and include your cell phone and scanner/radio with extra batteries or charger.

Depending on the shelter they may have a no weapons policy or size limits on knife blades. Keep this in mind when heading out. They will ask, I don't tell.

Leaving by car, put all of your nonperishable food and water in the trunk or out of site, you don't want others trying to break into your car to get at your food. If room permits take a change of clothes, some blankets or sleeping bag and something to do or read, along with a knife, multitool, flashlight and cell phone.

The best auto to drive is the one with the fullest fuel tank or highest ground clearance hopefully it will be one in the same. The vehicle with the fullest fuel tank if you will be driving a good distance or possibly at idle for a long time, using your vehicle to run the a/c or heat to stay comfortable, using your vehicle to charge cell phones, tablets or to run laptops with a inverter. The vehicle with the highest ground clearance is for when you have to go around/over/through something or most likely you need to cross a curb or sidewalk.

Driving a pickup? Have a chainsaw and some chain? Be sure to take these with you. Cutting your way through and/or dragging stuff out of the way may be the only way to get through.

Off site storage

Another idea or option if you don't have the ability to keep things secure or live with people that don't understand your desire to be prepared.

Rent a storage locker at one of the self storage places.

If this is to be your primary storage location, check elevation with GPS(protect against flooding), can you access your storage unit if the power is out (some have electric keypads and gates), do you need it close enough to access on foot, or is it on the way to your bug out location.....

Things to consider, is it climate controlled? Do you need power? Do you have to carry stuff down a hallway(possibility of people seeing what you are storing), or can you pull your vehicle right up to the door?

Different types of heat

When the power is out you won't have heat from your heat pump or forced air furnace.

If your home has propane or natural gas service you may have a small wall heating unit or gas logs that don't require electricity to operate. These generally cost around $200 for the unit of your choice plus installation. Having one of these in your home will make life much better in cold weather. While a small one may have trouble heating a whole house, just close off any rooms or closets that you don't need and throw an extra blanket on the bed and all will be OK.

Small propane heaters that work off of small disposable cylinders are a little on the small side for heating a whole house, they can be useful if you are only are trying to heat one room. Read the box carefully as some are not for use indoors. Look for low oxygen detector and auto shut off features, make sure it's suitable for use indoors.

Kerosene heaters are the easiest and simplest choice they come in two types generally referred to as round and square. The round ones put out a lot of heat and can easily heat up to a 1000 square feet. The downside is to refill you'll need to pick up a 20-30 pound heater and carry it outside to safely refill it and then carry it back inside full of kerosene.

Don't forget the hand pump to transfer kerosene from the container to the heater.

The square kerosene heaters (actually they are rectangular) put out about 2/3's the amount of the heat as a round unit. Most of them come with a removable fuel tank so you don't have to carry the whole unit outside to refill.

When purchasing a kerosene heater have a look at the top of the kerosene heater and see if it will support about 3-5lbs. The kerosene heaters that I have used and a quick check at the local home improvement store and local mega store all had the ability to support a pot of water on top. While it won't give you a rolling boil it will make the water steaming hot, which is good enough for heating up soup or making a cup of noodles.

When using a kerosene heater as a simple cook surface use pots with heat resistant handles, preferably metal handles, because the heat is not concentrated at the bottom of the pot. You are cooking on top of something that is designed to heat whole rooms. Be sure to use a hot pot holder.

Communications

Cell phones, I have had good luck with cell phones when my land line is not working, since a downed power pole also brings down your land line and cable TV.

After the last power outage I did some checking and found out that some cell phone towers have a back up power source and that most cell phones may be able to reach different cell towers automatically. You may have seen your cell phone doing this when it gives you a message "searching for service" what's its doing is checking for a cell tower with a available signal.

CB's good for 1-4 miles range depending on antenna location, higher is always better. Just flip through the channels and listen for anyone talking. Start with channel 19 its sort of a community chat channel. No license required cost $20-$80 + antenna.

Ham radio, usually the easiest way to find a ham radio operator is look for a house with some huge looking TV antenna's or antennas that look out of place as ham's use different types of antennas depending in the type of radio's they have. Ham radio does require a license from the FCC. Ham radios can cost $150.00 and up. Range depends on the license of the individual it can be from local to worldwide.

Scanner, with a scanner you can only listen, the good part is you can listen to CB (26.965-27.405mhz, ch.19 is 27.185mhz), ham radio (144-148mhz, 420-450mhz these are the most popular areas), NOAA weather channels (162.550, 162.400, 162.475, 162.425, 162.450, 162.500, 162.525 you may have to listen to several channels until you find the one that covers your area), fire, rescue, and police (150-420mhz, 450mhz and up).

If your scanner doesn't come with a 12 volt car plug in I would recommend one and a set of rechargeable batteries to fit your scanner or an extra battery pack if yours uses a battery pack. No license required. $125.00 and up.

Hand crank radio, just what it says, you crank a handle to generate power. Crank the handle for 2-3 minutes and you get up to 30 minutes of power. The one I have has a built in LED flashlight and an outlet for charging a cell phone with a special adapter. Look for a radio that picks up AM / FM / TV / NOAA weather stations. $10.00-$80.00.

GPS units

A global position system receiver is commonly known as a GPS. Tells you where you are at that time and the relative location of the things around you. Depending on the model and price is to how much detail about your surroundings you get. Translation higher cost equal's more details about your surroundings such as roads, lakes, hospitals, etc.

The models I have used all had elevation (or altitude) above sea level. If you intend to purchase one for this flooding or rising water exercise I would verify this feature is easy to access on the model you are interested in before purchase.

What I do is walk around my yard and up and down the street looking for the elevation of various spots or area's. See the following examples.

1. Lowest elevation point in my yard. 687'

2. Highest elevation point in my yard. 692'

3. Elevation of my porch or deck that is close to level with inside floor. 695'

4. Elevation of lowest point visible from my house or porch. 684'

5. Elevation of nearest river or creek with year round flowing water. 679'

From these numbers I can see that from the creek level (679') to the in the house level (695') is 16' that the water will have to rise. Now since the creek is about 2 blocks away and not visible from my porch I can look toward the lowest point visible from my porch (684') and tell that the water has risen 5' already and its got 11' more to go before it gets in the house. Now if I wake up and see water up to the low point in the yard (687') I know it's only got to rise another 5' before I can't drive out my driveway which is also the highest spot in my yard. Next plan your escape route out using the "high road".

Once you have completed surveying you immediate surroundings the next thing is to plan your escape route. Set the GPS on the dash of your auto and drive to your emergency shelter (fire station, hospital, friends or family). As you drive along note if at any point along your route the elevation is lower than the elevations visible from your home. When you get to your planned shelter check the elevation to see if it's higher (safer) or lower (bad) than your home.

In my area the fire station and hospital are both 20-25 feet lower than my home. While the local church is 30 feet higher in elevation than my home and less than 1 mile away if you cross the river that's subject to flooding, I solved this by the use of my GPS and found a way around using some back roads and cutting though a housing development so that at all times I am at least 20 feet above the elevation of the nearest creek, however this route is a little over 6 miles long.

Flooding

As soon as you become aware of impending flooding get ready to leave. Pack the vehicle with the highest ground clearance and follow your "high road" route to safety.

Don't drive through water if you can't see the lines on the road through the water. If you can't see the roadway there is no way to tell if its still there or washed away. If you are in a situation where you are having to push your luck, take or wear something that floats such as life preservers, ski vests, floating cushions, pool toys, coolers, tire inner tubes, footballs, basketballs or anything that will float and help keep your head above water.

Before you leave put any thing you can't take with you such as irreplaceable pictures and such in waterproof containers and put as high as possible in your home, on top of the refrigerator or in the attic.

Didn't have time to prepare for the high road? Look for multi level parking garages, drive on in and up, and claim you a parking space. If the parking garage is several stories high try not to get on the very top level the sun will cook you. Look for water towers these are generally built in an area with a higher elevation to save the city on pumping costs.

Guns

The power is out, why would I want a gun? If the power is out due to natural causes such as localized severe weather or someone hit a power pole with their car. You can expect power crews to be working on restoring power as soon as practical. In which case a firearm would not be needed.

In the case of a widespread disaster or a terrorist attack, lines of communication may not be working or the emergency services may be totally overwhelmed and emergency calls will get prioritized by importance. If there is any widespread flooding, looting, rioting, a major fire or explosions you may not even see an officer respond to your call for a couple of days.

That being said, what is the best gun for someone that doesn't know anything about guns, for the protection of yourself and your home? The overwhelming preferred choice is a .38 special (caliber and cartridge size) double action revolver with a 2" barrel and if you can afford it, upgrade to the chrome or stainless finish. This gives them better resistance to rust and corrosion. Also shown in the picture above is a .38/.357 with a 6" barrel. Expect to pay $200 -$500

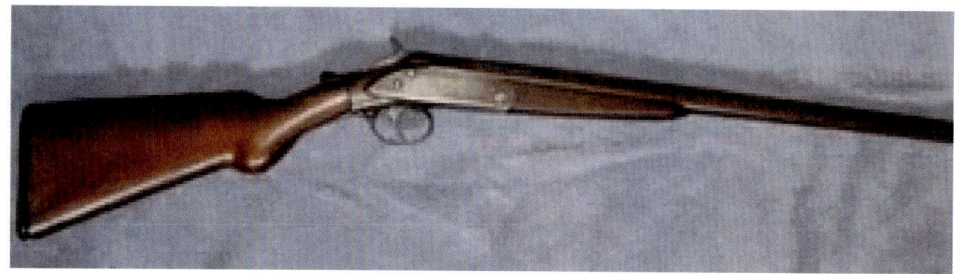

The next choice is a single barrel break open shot gun in 20 gauge or 12 gauge. The 20 ga. Is the smaller of the two, it is also excellent for small game such as doves, rabbits and squirrels. The 12ga. shotgun is a universal gun that can also be used for small game and larger game such as deer. The 12 ga. does recoil with more force against your shoulder. I would recommend you find someone with both a 20 ga. and a 12ga. and will let you fire a couple of rounds of both before you make your purchase.

Both gauges offer a variety of shot sizes for small game hunting (#8-#5) to buck shot for larger game. Single barrel shotgun prices are $100-$250

If you don't know anyone look in the phone book under gun range, some offer basic gun safety courses and will let you rent different types of guns owned by the gun range. Don't be shy about telling them you don't know anything and your purpose for the visit to their range.

You can also call the gun stores and ask about local gun ranges and a basic gun safety course. There are gun safety courses and hunter safety courses. The gun safety course or training is designed to teach you how to handle firearms in a safe manner to prevent you from shooting a hole in something or someone accidentally. The hunter safety course will also cover gun safety, rules for the hunt and may be required before your allowed to purchase a hunting license. There are also concealed carry courses taught which are more advanced and expect you to have a good proficiency with your handgun, as a portion of the course is a live fire exercise. The concealed carry courses are generally more about the when and why's of self defense.

The first rule of gun safety is don't point a gun at something unless you plan on shooting it.

The second rule of gun safety is keep your finger off the trigger until your ready to shoot.

It is your responsibility (the reader) to determine the gun laws in your area. It is also your responsibility find out the law as to when you have the right to use deadly force to protect yourself or your property.

I would not recommend any type of semi-automatic hand gun for your first gun. Semi-auto's must be kept clean and can show a dislike for certain kinds of ammo, and the last thing you want is a gun to jam when it's your life on the line. If your interested in a semi-automatic gun make sure that all individuals that will be using it have the hand strength to pull the slide back and can clear a stove pipe jam. A stove pipe jam can be demonstrated in the store without a problem.

Also when you call the gun store, ask how to purchase a gun in your state, some states have waiting periods, some have permits for handguns only, some have permits for hand and long guns, some have no waiting with an instant FBI background check.

Cash, credit, or trade?

When the power is out all electronic transactions come to a halt. I do still carry my credit card when going out to purchase gas, groceries or water as some stores use satellite communications and have their own generators. Be sure and ask before pumping a tank full of gas or have a buggy full of groceries.

Cash is cash good for all debts public and private anywhere in the United States and some foreign countries.

Trade or barter, if the power is out the local ATM may not be working and your bank may or may not be open. What can I use for trade? The most common items in my experience were cigarettes, beer/alcohol, toilet paper, candy bars (chocolate), food items, instant coffee, gas, kerosene, clothing, and condoms.

I try to avoid trading or giving away drinkable water, if my neighbors, friends or family need to flush a commode and my rain barrels are full I'll give them enough for their use.

I don't trade away ammunition or guns. This always concerns me when someone is looking for guns or ammo in a survival situation. On the other hand if it's my neighbors that I know and trust along with looting or riots in the area, this is a "you watch my back I'll watch yours" kind of deal.

Car Food Kit

When making a Food stash for the car, I put some water and granola bars in a small cooler(remember a cooler is a insulated box designed to keep the internal temperature stable). So far I have tested this with overnight temperatures down to 20 degrees without the water freezing. With it being in a cooler if it did manage to freeze and burst its still in what amounts to a bucket so it won't leak as long as its kept upright. I also put in snacks wrapped in plastic wrappers in case a water bottle does leak I can still eat them.

This kit has 5 bottles of water and about 20 chewy snack bars and breakfast bars, tuck a warm blanket in the trunk of your car and you could survive a night on the side of a road.

How to figure foodstuffs and how much to keep.

When purchasing extra foodstuffs, stay with food you normally eat.

When thinking about keeping an extra months food in the house the first thing that comes to mind is a prepper preparing for SHTF. What if you got laid off for 2-3 weeks with no income, that's a very real SHTF for everybody I know.

Before, when I would go to the grocery store I would generally buy the same thing every week and only buy enough for the week.

Now that I realized that I needed to keep extra, all I had to do was buy a few extra items each week (my budget was about $30 for the extra) and after about a month and a half I had enough to live on for a month with no problems.

If you normally buy 2 cans/boxes/bags of something every week, next week buy 4. When u get home put the new items in behind the items you already had, to keep your supplies rotated. It's that easy.

Everything I buy has a date on it, after a while you will notice that most items have a expired date that's about a year away. Dry foods may have two years till they expire. I've bought Spam and treet (canned meats) that is good for three years. If I can't understand the date code on a food item I won't buy it.

To give you a idea of how much canned food you need, I use this as a starting point, a can with meat in it and a can of vegetables per meal per person. Which works out to 6 cans of food per day per person, plus I like to add in a can of fruit as a treat for a total of 7 cans of food per day. If your feeding big eaters you can figure 9-12 cans per day.

I figure it by the can, because I'm assuming you have no way to keep food refrigerated once it has been opened in a power out situation. Once the can of food is opened it is to be eaten by you or a member of your family or group. Remember CANNED food is cooked or pasteurized as part of the canning process and can be eaten cold. It may not taste as good, but you won't be hungry.

Everything on this list is already in my house all I had to do is get some extra.

-Bottled water 1gal jugs and/or cases of small 16oz water bottles (1 gal per day per person as a minimum)

-Granola bars,

-Dry breakfast cereal,

-Quaker oats, I get the kind that comes 12 packs to a box and just add hot water.

-Canned vegetables,

-Canned fruit,

-Tea, Instant coffee, 1 jar lasts me a week, 4 jars and I'm good for a month, it's that easy

-100% fruit juices either bottled or boxed,

-Canned meats, tuna, chicken, ham (usually have a 1-2 year expiration date)

-Canned spam, treet, corned beef hash (I have seen these with expire dates 3-4 years out)

-pasta and spaghetti sauce in jars or cans

-canned soups

-canned Chef Boyardee meals

-Peanut butter

-Crackers, Saltines,Ritz

-Pedialyte/Gatorade,

-Ramen noodles, not the greatest food but they are cheap and only need boiling water.

-Hard candy

-Powdered milk or shelf stable milk (can be stored for 6 months without refrigeration)

-Salt, sugar, I prefer to buy small sizes or packs so I don't risk having it in one place.

-Packaged snacks, little Debbie cakes, cheese and crackers

Non food items

-Lighters, grill lighters with the extended handle.

-manual Can openers get several

-Toilet paper with four people in a house it's common to go through a roll a day.

-Soap, hand sanitizer, mouth wash

-Medicines, rubbing alcohol, band aids, peroxide, antibiotics for cuts, etc.

-Extra propane tank or charcoal for your grill, so you can cook or heat water.

Don't forget your pets. Figure water and food. A half a bottle of water tops off the cats water dish the other half I drink. In our house a 7 pound bag of cat food lasts 8 days and that's feeding 3 cats, a bucket of cat litter lasts 2 weeks. For a month I need 28 pounds of cat food and 2 extra buckets of cat litter.

3 cases of water, about 12 gallons total. That's enough for 2 people for 5-6 days. Total cost $11

The simplest way of explaining it, keep your cabinets FULL with food you WILL NORMALLY EAT. If you will notice I buy canned vegetables, canned meats, dried milk and shelf stable milk that doesn't need refrigeration.

Don't have a lot of cabinet space? Try a small shelf in the back of a closet.

Food storage and shelf life guidelines

The following is a partial list of foods and how long they are good, past their expire dates. This list is used by the local food banks. A complete list is available as a download from www.foodshare.org it's approximately 12 pages long. All dates are based on the product being unopened in its original container.

When using foods past their expiration date, your senses are usually the most reliable guide to tell you if something is bad. If it smells bad, it is. Has mold? It's too old.

Canned goods

Acid-based products...........18 months past date on can
(tomato based products, fruits, sauerkraut, foods in vinegar-based sauces)

Soups..........3 years past date on can
(other than tomato based)

Vegetables..........3 years past date on can

Jelly and Jams..........1 year past date on can

Peanut Butter..........1 year past date on can

Canned Meats..........18 months past date on can

Tuna and Chicken **_pouches_**..........9 months past date on pouch

Tuna **_lunch kits_**..........Must be in date

Milk..........Must be in date
(evaporated/condensed)

Milk..........6 months past date on product
(dried/powdered)

Grain Products

Boxed Breakfast Cereal..........8 months past date on box

Hot Cereal..........6 months past date on box
(Oatmeal, Cream of Wheat, Grits)

Breakfast and Granola Bars..........8 months past date on box

Pop-tarts..........1 year past date on box

Crackers and Cookies..........6 months past dates on box

Snack cakes..........MUST be in date

Flour and Cornmeal..........6 months past date on box

Baking mixes..........6 months past date on box
(cake, brownies, pancake, cornbread)

Pasta – Rice – Dried beans

Pasta..........1 year past date on product
(spaghetti, noodles, etc.)

Macaroni and cheese..........1 year past date on product

Rice (white)..........2 years past date on product
Rice (mixed)..........6 months past date on product

Instant Rice..........2 months past date on product

Dry beans..........1 year past date on product

Dry soup mix..........1 year past date on product

Beverages

Soda..........6 months past date on product

Diet Soda..........3 months past date on product

Juice.........3 months past date on product

Juice boxes..........3 months past date on product

Bottled Water..........1 year past date on product

Hot chocolate Mix..........2 years past date on product

Coffee..........2 years past date on product

Tea.........2 years past date on product

Mixes..........1 year past date on product

(Kool-aid, tang, etc.)

Condiments

Ketchup..........3 months past date on product

Mayonnaise..........3 months past date on product

Salad dressing..........6 months past date on product
*Ranch dressing..........3 months past date on product

Mustard, pickles, syrup, vinegar, cooking oil.......... 1 year past date on product

Sauces..........1 year past date on product
(steak sauce, BBQ sauce, etc.)

Other items

Sugar
granulated...........2 years past date on product
brown..........2 years past date on product
powdered..........18 months past date on product

Jello / pudding cups..........2 months past date on product

Dried fruit..........6 months past date on product

Potato chips, pretzel, etc...........6 months past date on product

How to tell if eggs are bad

Many people use the egg float test. Although it is not 100% accurate, it allows you to tell if an egg is bad without cracking the shell. If you wonder if your egg has gone bad, simply submerge it in water to test if the egg has expired. A good egg will sink to the bottom and stay there on its side. An egg that stands with its larger side up is older, but the egg is still good. If the egg floats or hovers, then bacteria have broken down proteins in the egg whites and created gases, an indication that the egg is probably unsafe to eat. This quick test may result in a false negative, but better safe than sorry and any egg that fails this test should be thrown out.

Honey

Did you know that honey lasts forever? It may crystallize with time, but it's one of nature's most perfect food, and great for home storage.

Emergency food for long term storage

MRE (Meal ready to eat)

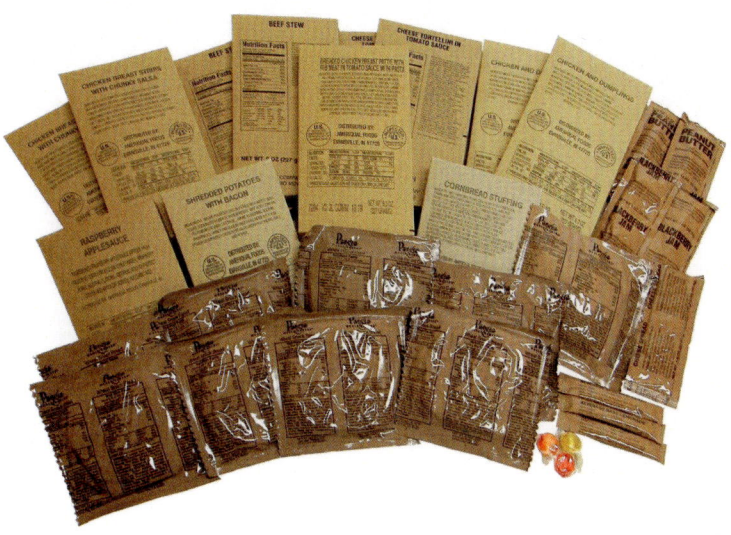

MRE Shelf Life

The MRE shelf life is typically a long period of time and they are also able to be in extreme temperatures without having any damage done to them, though the higher the temperature, the shorter the MRE will last. According to the U.S. Army's Natick Research Laboratory, MREs kept at 70 degrees can last about 100 months, or a little over eight years.

Some of the MRE's are not suitable for people on salt or fat restricted diet.

As long as conditions and the environment around them is stable, MREs will last a rather long time. Many continue to taste fine up to five years after date of packaging. Additionally, when you take the time and care to store them properly, they are not going to attract bugs or pests of any type.

MRE Heater

Make sure when buying MRE's kits, that they come with a heater!!!!! Some brands do not include the heater so they can sell them cheaper. MRE's can also be heated by putting them in hot water for a few minutes.

When you have MRE meals for an emergency kit, you are going to need a way to heat your meals and that is where a MRE heater can help you out. A MRE heater is simply a small bag that is used to heat your meals and you simply add water or any other type of liquid and the bag is aluminum lined. The magnesium that is at the bottom of the bags heats the liquid and this allows you to heat up your MRE meals. You will be able to enjoy hot meals even in emergency or disaster situations.

What Kind of MRE Meals Are Available?

In regards to what is included in an MRE meal, there is a wide variety. You can find them in a few different ways including MRE full meals, MRE entrees, MRE snacks, Cases of MRE meals(generally have heaters included, double check this when purchasing)

As far as what is in the case, you get your choice of an entree, your choice of snacks, a drink mix, deserts, condiments, and heating pouches to heat your meals in.

Can be found at almost any army surplus store, Amazon, or camping supply store.

Freeze dried food

Freeze dried food can be purchased as meals, individual food items or by the case/bucket. Cases and buckets are generally 9-27 meals, may also include a couple of extra items such as heaters for boiling water or extra packages of sweet items. Easy to heat just add hot water directly into the bag. Generally have at least a 5 year shelf life, I have seen some with a 10 year shelf life.

Freeze dried food may also be bought by the can with a 25 year, yes that said 25 year shelf life. These are normally a large #10 can containing 8-10 servings per can. $18-$30 per can, these are the best deal if you need to feed a family. The only downside is that once the can is opened it needs to be eaten with in a week or so, if your feeding a family this should not be a problem.

I think these are the easiest foods to store, they are light weight, packed in a heavy grade of Mylar plastic, have a long shelf life and I think they(mountain house brand) taste much better than MRE's. The best part is when they get close to the expiration, just eat them. They're just like a regular meal that happens to be freeze dried. This gives you practice and a meal. Can be expensive if bought individually, $5-$8 per individual meal.

I the ones I have tried used 1-2 cups of hot water and you wait 5-10 minutes for the food to heat and rehydrate, add a fork or spoon and your ready to eat. Not all freeze dried foods need to be heated. some of the packs that only have a single type of fruit can be eaten just by adding cold water to the package.

I normally order these from Amazon by the bucket which gets the per package price down to around $6 per meal, I have also found them at Walmart in the camping section and some large outdoor stores.

Emergency food bars and water

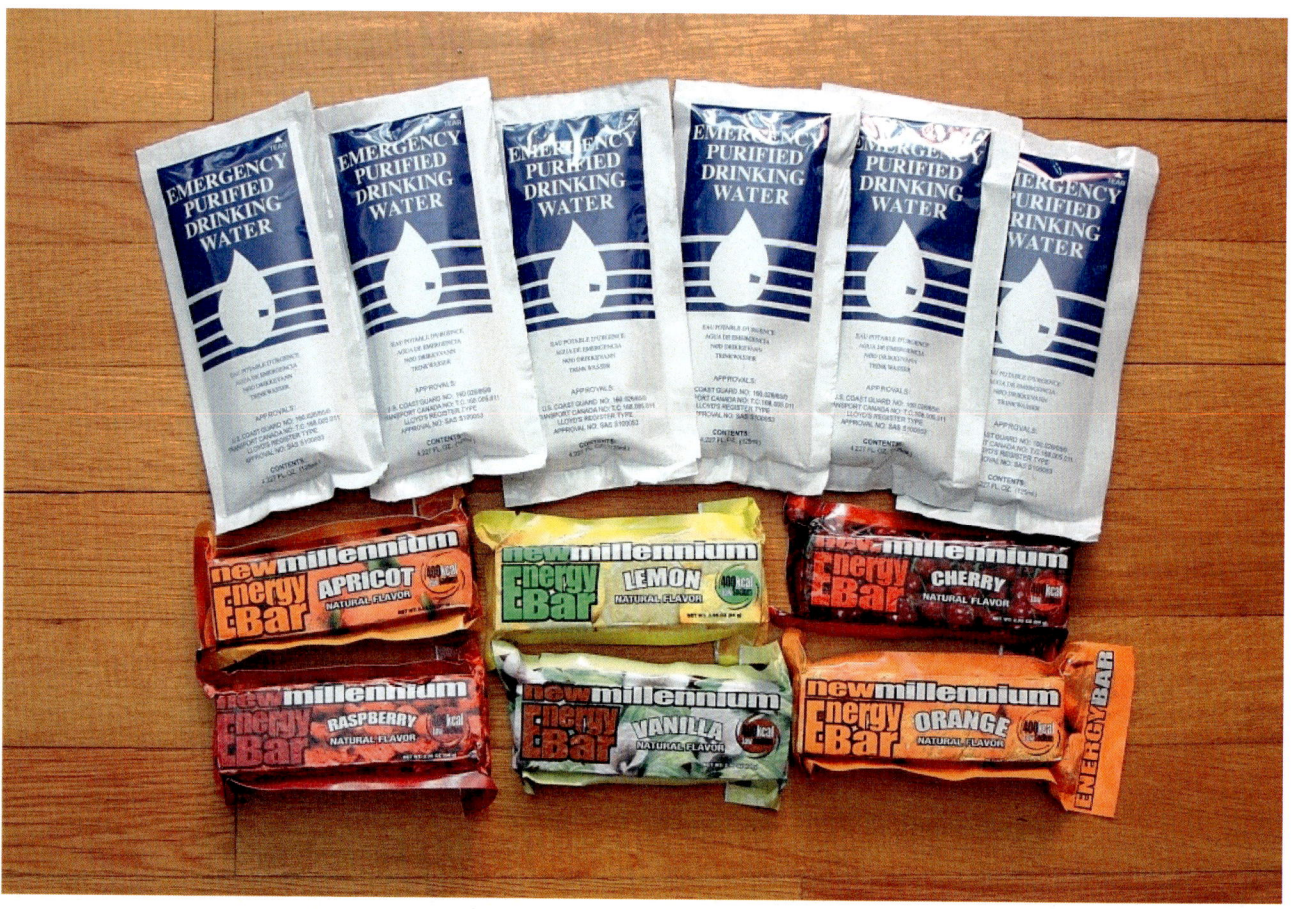

Your on the side of the road waiting for a tow truck, it's 11:00am, all you had for breakfast at 6:00am was a cup of coffee and a bagel, now your feeling weak and your throat is dry and it's going to be a hot summer day. Eat a survival bar and a emergency packet of water and you'll be OK.

Emergency Drinking Water Packets. Purified and bacteria free water products. Unlike bottled water which must be rotated and replaced every 6 months, these water packets last for up to 5 years. Water ration pouches can withstand temperatures ranging from -40° F to 230° F. Can be frozen without any adverse effects. Water is also extremely important to insure that your mind (your greatest survival tool) continues to work well because even a small degree of dehydration adversely affects your ability to think. 12 pack of emergency water from Amazon is $6.49 for a three day supply. Each pouch is 4.227 oz/125 ml

Having a survival food bar can come in handy in different situations as it keeps well in varying storage temperatures. Usually, these bars can be stored in between a temperature range of -40 to 300 degrees Fahrenheit. Emergency bars are also packed to be waterproof and lightproof. Most bars have a shelf life of 5 years, making these lightweight but nutrition-packed foods a necessity in survival food kits.

Are Emergency Food Bars Enough to Replace Three Meals a Day?

These food bars contain a lot of protein, vitamins, and minerals as it is designed to provide the same basic nutrients you would expect to get from a regular meal. Three emergency bars will usually provide the body with 1200 calories which is enough to support one's daily calorie needs. Emergency bars usually come in packs of 9 so 1 box will be able to give you 3 days of emergency food supplies. It is not advisable though to eat emergency bars everyday for a long-term basis but nevertheless, these bars provide security in case regular food cannot be obtained.

All of these could be ordered for around $8-$20 each. I believe that's a great deal for a 3 day supply of food, remember these are designed to keep you alive in a bad situation and be stored for long periods of time, up to 5 years.

Types of Food Bars

There are different brands of food bars in the market. Some may consider emergency bars as the last resort but it pays to know which food bars are most suitable for your taste in case of emergencies. Food bars come in different package size, caloric value, and flavors.

New Millennium, come in cherry, orange, vanilla, lemon, raspberry, apricot flavors and are packed individual in 400 calorie bars. I buy these in 24 piece assorted packs for $30 from Amazon.

The following types all came packed with several bars in one pack, once they are opened you have to use the whole package or throw away the part you don't need.

Mayday Emergency Food Bars, have an apple cinnamon flavor.

Mainstay Emergency Food Bars, Mainstay food bars are lemon flavored.

Datrex Emergency Bars, Datrex bars have a coconut flavor.

S.O.S. Rations Emergency Bars, Coconut flavor

I recommend ordering and trying several kinds of survival food bars. There are other kinds and flavors, these are just the ones I have tried.

Where to Find Survival Food

You can find survival food for sale online, Amazon and camping supply websites and in some grocery stores.

Planting fruit trees and gardening

Storing 30 days of food is a good goal. But you'll run out of food if there's a prolonged disaster. Many people think, if I run out of food I'll just go hunting. Keep in mind, you'll be hunting just like everyone else in town, so the supply of wild game will be thinned out quickly. So you implement a self sustaining food supply. Turn your yard into a edible landscape.

Gardens and orchards are both part of the solution. Gardens generally tend to include annuals whereas orchards provide food year after year. Storing heirloom seeds for your garden, will enable you to grow food quickly, and after each harvest store store some seeds for the next year. You should be aware that many commercially sold seeds will produce vegetables with sterile seeds, this is intentional, Commercial seed producers want you to buy their patented seeds year after year. In a SHTF world this is a problem.

Heirloom seeds yield vegetables with fertile seed so you can save some to replant the following years and that's important for continued survival.

Gardening is good , but it's also very labor intensive. If you've never grown a garden you may be surprised to learn it can be very difficult. This learning curve can be overcome with a clear gardening plan. Research which plants grow best in you area. Do you have a clay or Acidic soil? Search the internet or call your agricultural agent to learn which crops grow best in your area.

 Consider replacing your inedible lawn with a small orchard of fruit trees, nut trees, and berry bushes. When planted, they'll produce food for the next 40 years or longer. A home orchard of 5-15 trees and berry bushes, will be a lot less work to take care of then a garden, and the yield of food generally increases with each and every passing year.

 Fruit trees, nut trees, and berry bushes are usually sold at plant nurseries, Home Depot, Lowe's, and ArborDay.org. The Arbor day website has a search tool (click on the "tree" tab) where you can enter your zip code and it will recommend the best trees and bushes for your area. At our local Lowes you can get apple, peach, pear, plum, fig, several different types of grapes, blueberry, strawberry and raspberry, ranging in price from $8-$20 per tree/bush. So for a $100 you could buy 3 fruit trees and a few berry bushes that will provide you with food for the next 40 years or longer. It does generally take 3-5 years before they start to produce a good quantity of fruit, but once they do you will be giving away fruit because there is no way to eat it all.

I choose to go to local nursery that has fruit trees that they have grown in this area, so that I would be assured of getting trees that will survive in our area. I told them I was looking for fruit trees and berry bushes that were low maintenance and the fruits could be eaten right off the plant. I picked out apple, peach, pear, perennial strawberries and 4 blueberry bushes for $150, add in a day of digging holes and your all done. A couple of things to remember is some fruit trees need to be planted in pairs (for example two apple trees) so they can cross pollinate this allows them to maximize fruit production, whereas the peaches I picked out can self pollinate so you only need one. When planting it was recommended to fill the hole about ½ way with water before putting in the tree and then watering again after you finished putting dirt around the tree.

When planting fruit trees plant them away from anything you don't want to have fruit falling on, once fruit trees are fully grown they produce a lot of fruit, more than you can ever eat. They will also attract rabbits, squirrels, birds and possibly deer depending on your location.

What if you don't have a big yard or no yard at all? Contact your local town/city hall to see if they might grant you permission to plant trees in one of the local parks. Some will, others will not, also ask neighbor's if you can plant on their land.

The reality is that asking for permission to grow on land doesn't always work. Which is why a new trend of guerrilla growing is becoming common among preppers. This is where preppers plant fruit trees, nut trees and berry bushes on parks or abandoned land near their homes. This type of growing is illegal. But for those who don't own land it might be the best option. Even preppers who own land will often guerrilla grow along their bug out route. They do this every few miles along their bug out route. In the event that they need to bug out, fresh food is available along their route.

Be aware that most online distributors of fruit trees ship only in early spring and late fall, because the trees are dormant and more likely to live.

Spending just one weekend to plant fruit and nut trees now, could benefit you for the next 50 years.

E.D.C duck tape

(E.D.C = Everyday Carry)

How to make a EDC duck tape key chain.

Items needed, small rope or cordage, duck tape, knife and a ruler.

Cut a 6" piece of cordage.

Unroll about 3 feet of duck tape and stick the cordage to it as shown in the following picture. I like to line up the cut ends of the cordage with the edge of the tape, I think it looks cleaner when finished.

Fold the duck tape over on itself. Try to get this part straight and tight, it will make rolling a lot easier.

Then roll slowly and carefully keeping the edge's lined up.

I put a little notch at the end, in case I only need a narrow piece for a small repair.

In the following picture the roll on the left is somewhat bigger then the rest, it has about 9 feet of duck tape while the others are 3 foot rolls. All of the rolls in the following picture took me about 20 minutes to make. As you can see there are many choice's in duck tape colors for the individuals that don't want to carry a gray duck tape key chain.

Hand line for fishing and kit

Items needed

some fishing line(15-20lb), duct tape, small rope or cordage, rubber bands/o-ring, a short piece of pvc pipe/bamboo/dowel rod

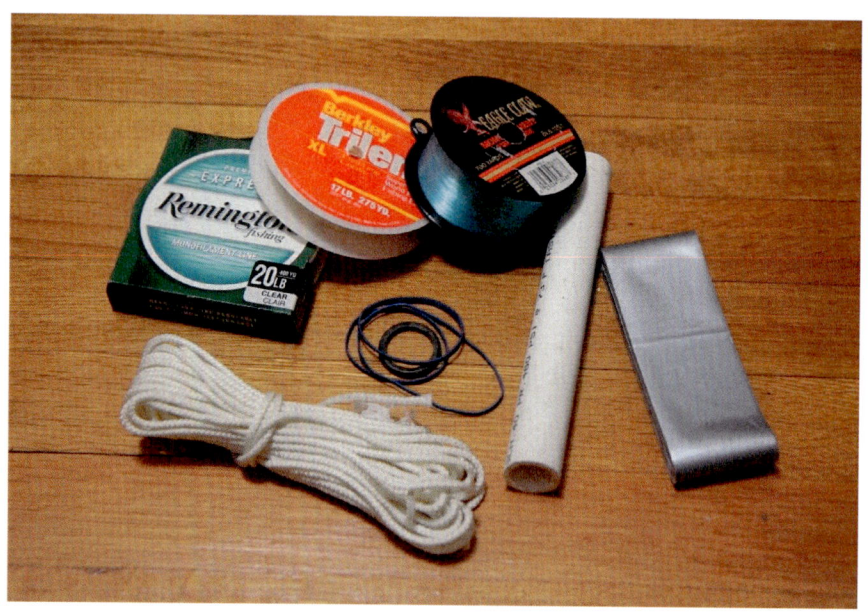

Drill a hole in one end, for the rope wrist strap.

Sand ends and edges smooth

Attach the fishing line with duct tape as shown.

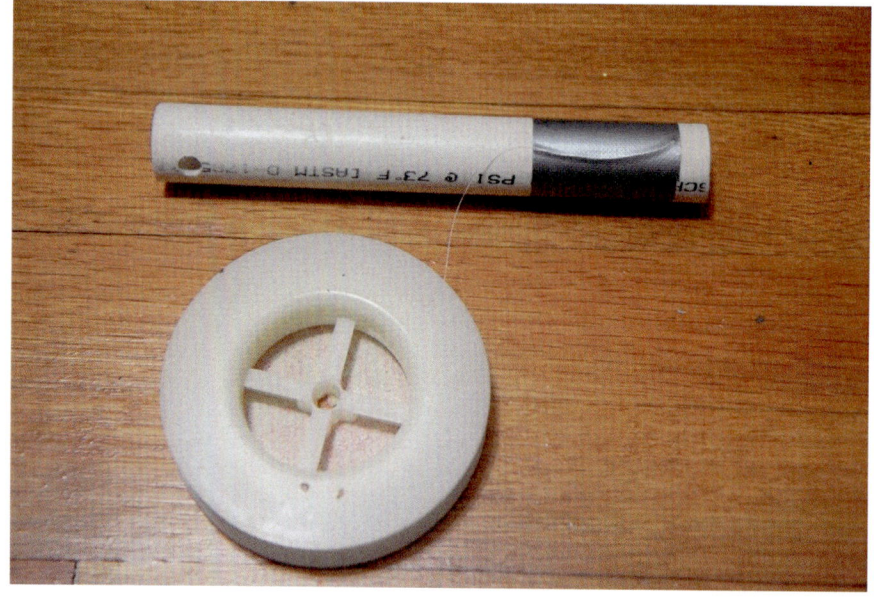

Then wind about 100 feet of line around the end. I hook the line as shown below and then walk about 30-35 steps(approx. 100") while holding the "fishing rod".

Then I cut the line free from the spool, before winding it on the "rod" this prevents the line from kinking up. When winding the line keep it on the duct tape.

Shown below is the "fishing rod" after the line has been wound around it and temporally secured with a rubber band to keep it from unraveling, I also slide the o-ring or rubber band on making sure they fit snug, then cut about 18-20" of cord for the wrist strap and install as shown.

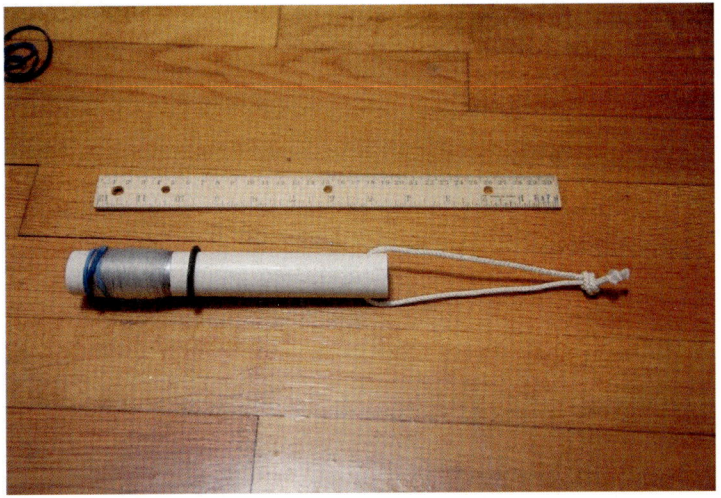

Attach a swivel hook to your line and tuck it under the o-ring as shown to keep the line from unraveling.

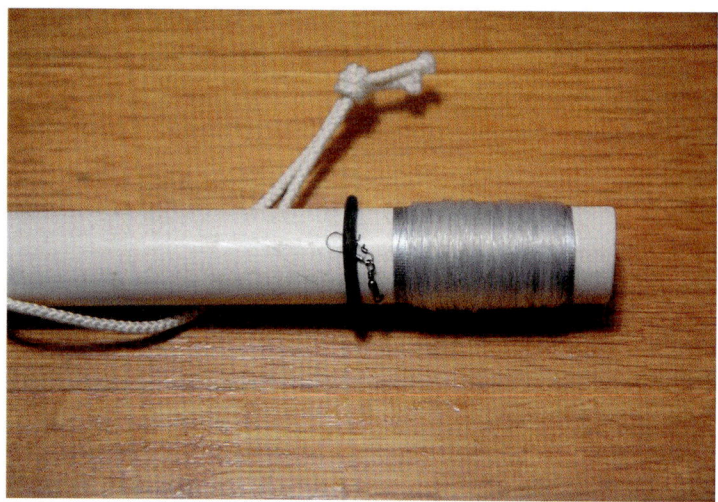

Completed "fishing rod" and a simple kit. Includes weighted floats some hooks, swivels, weights and 10' of duct tape around the pill bottle/tackle storage.

All packed and ready to go.

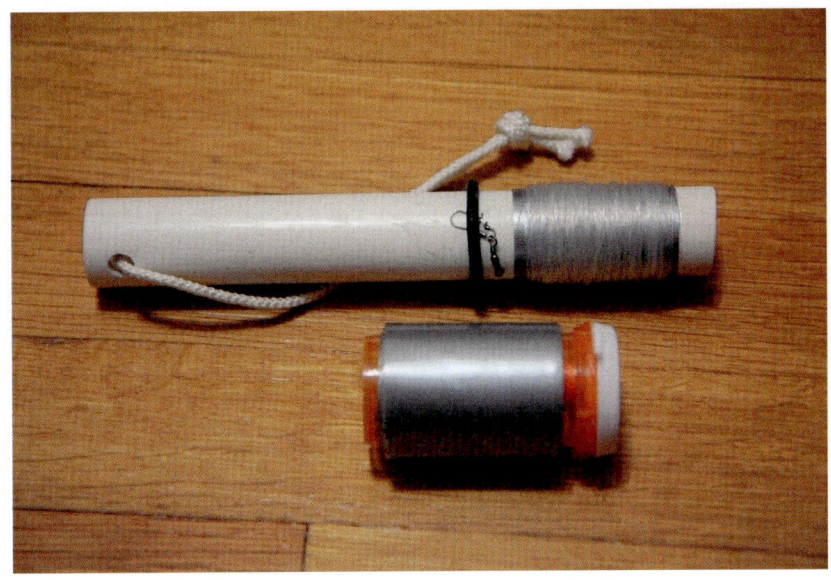

Shown below, I put together a small kit for fishing.

You may also notice I wrapped the "fishing rod" handle with some cord. I have tried using duct tape around the handle, but it has a tendency to get very sticky on the palm of your hand.

THANK YOU FOR READING "WHEN THE LIGHTS GO OUT"

THE END

Made in the USA
Middletown, DE
22 June 2017